T0113609

Between Places:

Poetry Journal

2017-2020

Tendai Rinos Mwanaka

Mwanaka Media and Publishing Pvt Ltd,
Chitungwiza Zimbabwe
*
Creativity, Wisdom and Beauty

Publisher:
Mwanaka Media and Publishing Pvt Ltd *(Mmap)*
24 Svosve Road, Zengeza 1
Chitungwiza Zimbabwe
mwanaka@yahoo.com
mwanaka13@gmail.com
www.africanbookscollective.com/publishers/mwanaka-media-and-publishing
https://facebook.com/MwanakaMediaAndPublishing/

Distributed in and outside N. America by African Books Collective
orders@africanbookscollective.com
www.africanbookscollective.com

ISBN: 978-1-77925-573-0
EAN: 9781779255730

DISCLAIMER
All views expressed in this publication are those of the author and do not necessarily reflect the views of *Mmap*.

TABLE OF CONTENTS

Introducing Between Places

To refuse yourself to feel things is to refuse yourself to breathe yet you are breathing. To be unaware of yourself breathing. To not know of the warmth and moistures of your breath. To not know of the human sounds of life. To refuse yourself to feel things is to not see the sky above the building across your windows. To hear noise below you as pollution. To refuse yourself to feel things is to live between places. To be in the east until it begins to feel like east, it takes you 4 seasons for you to figure out where the sun is coming from and going back to come back at that same position, but before the fourth season, you found yourself to the west. Sekelgrass music is lost to the sounds of traffic passing through Sekelgras road off to…you don't know. To refuse yourself is to live for a month in the west and move to the centre, to see a person and not to talk to them. To see a spirit that sees you not. In a matchbox abdomen, you refuse to call this home. Before the west becomes the sounds and vowels that you use to describe home, the horizons trails off as you move to the centre. But the actual events happened vice versa, west to east…but we all know we artistically would start with east to west to lend credence to the theory of the eastern myth. Don't sweat! It is what it has become…the centre. To refuse to feel things is to stay in the centre that doesn't hear you, yet like the heart it should, must hear you. You know the centre has lived inside you for a year now, you still don't hear it, it doesn't hear you too. It doesn't see you. To live between places is to be a fish that learns to live out of water to learn the first word of its alphabet. To refuse to feel anything is to refuse to hear the last gasp of a dying fish denied of its earth. To live between places is to subtract everything until even a negative is not a number. That's the primary school of living between places, it's like 1 minus 2 equals *it cant!*

WATER IS LIFE

As present as memory
Water is our lifeline
Like memory,
It doesn't care for borders, boundaries.
The highest precision for wings,
It is everywhere
Water is spiritual
The silence of our ritual departing
I hear the call for water
I hear the call inside me
Water is who we are
We can live without food
Jesus, Moses, John The Baptist, in the desert
The daily bread was beyond their breakfasts
Trust me, we can tell this, or not
We can live without a lot of things
But some truths are ours alone
We cannot live without water
Water is why, when-
The grass wears its skirts of dew
A bionic vision of loving
That binds the natural world of life
In it everything crackles, gleams, shimmers,
Hums, explodes with life like a ghetto street
Water in her veins, nourishing
Our first Mother, Earth

Grows her plants healthily
Life goes in a circle
Water connects the circles
Rest is not rest- it is urgency
Water teaches us about change
Re-imagines the world through dreams
A struggle with eternal death
And of different seasons
Water in a mother's womb
Her aims are helpful and compassionate
She is here. She is life
That bag of water that
Overlooks the marketplace of human life
Protects, nourishes, starts it all
Right there, accessible to all
Water that comes from the sky
Water that comes from the river, streams, lakes
Water that comes from underground, oceans
Water that comes from the eyes
Water that comes from the breasts
Water that comes in blood, in sweat, in wet
Water that cleanses, nourishes, grows
Care for this water
Speak for this water
Pray for this water
Dance for this water
Bless for this water
Sing for this water
Talk for this water

Teach for this water
Cry for this water
Don't put this in the "maybe" file
Put this in the "save" file
Don't let half of the "save" file
Become "miscellaneous bin" in the garage of your soul
Listen to this fateful rap on the door of our undoing
Oh, we can say we were (are) sorry
But that future never takes it back to now.

6 September 2017

He is in bed, 10 o'clock, cocks the morning
Mourning hymn-hums of a refrigerator soaks,
Knocks the room with humming music, of soft horns
He is droning into the hymns of the hums
Of(f)ish his mind, his skull skulks the skies
Of white matter, it doesn't matter
The chatter outside, deciding into the sides
Inside the walls of his closed room,
That rooms a wardrobe, sideboard, hoards
Of clutter homes every corner, clicks
Pans, spoons, clangs inside the walls
Of his mind, close to cooking, he closes
Into the sheets, in these cotton skins
He finds the skin he lives inside of
He has lived in this skin, skull, caulk
For over seven years, months, days, none-
Tendai-tee shirteeing his name out of this room
Outside the room, the dulled explosions
Of songbirds in his brain's lymphatic nodes,
Rides to the music of his grey matter
It doesn't matter, he doesn't see this outside
He is in bed, 12 o'clock, locks the noons
No one is in this room with him, only the music
Of Tracy Chapman, "These arms... Open arms...
Time is what you need..." *dindi tinditi tindititi*
To do what? He is in bed alone- a lone light
Lights loneliness so bereft, he only

Feels its heat in the crosshairs of his cotton
Skins, that masks air with the musk
Of his grey matter, it doesn't matter
The explosions, implosions, inside plosions…
Plosives, corrosives, and invasive animals that corrodes
Cuts, jabs, jibs; incisions into small sizes;
And seizures his mind- an orgy organism.
He is in his bed, and it's after 12 o'clock
After 12, after what, after when, afar, far
The silent drones of traffics in the city's
Black arteries, veins, nodes, nodes past, stops
The noise stoops the fissures of his thoughts
Jagged dreamscapes that haunts his days
And nights, he backs into last night's dream
Warpy worlds of self-accusations, the runs
Selfishly, self-saving himself from his monsters
Hubris, inkling, inking the dark Wolds of
Swords angling towards him, to wade, to
Duck in, to dive, to die, to death's…
To defy his black tentacles, grey smoky fangs
He is in bed, its 1 o'clock, clocking hunger
He stops this mind. He looks for what can be eaten
In this room inside the greys in his mind

******

When hunger guts him, his mind unbefriends working.
He feels like the pangs of hunger are gnawing his
spleens, his brain, his nerves. So, he pours himself a

drink, Stoner Ginger Beer, yes its written "beer". He has teased his cousin he stays with, that they were drinking beer. They don't drink beer. Stone ginger beer never gets anyone drunk, does it? A beer that doesn't gets one drunk, drunk by people who don't drink (beer), with rice and some pieces.., of pork chops. He loves… food. Food is art that can be eaten. Art has to be that delectable like food. It has to be eaten. Eating is harmless fun, if you eat well. Eating spaghetti and meatballs, eating sadza and goat's meat, eating Nhopi and Rupiza… his intention is to make you pine for food! He is a seductress, with his art!

He bleeds the afternoon hours socializing on
Facebook, WhatsApp, Instagram, Twitter, twitting
Off the birds outside, it's warm-womb spring here
Yet in posts, calls, huffs, anger, disgust
His American friends mourn, Harvey and Irma-
Names of crooked monsters, cooked by angry sea gods
Unleashed on the American stomachs-
Devastating, Destroying, Decapitating, killing… D bears some words, word… you don't want on you

In the Shona language there is an expression for what's happening to his American friends, "Mai votsva musana mwana votsva dumbu" literary meaning a "mother burns on the back whilst the child burns on the stomach." It happens with the act of carrying, when a mother carries a baby on her back. The friction and

6

heat between the back and stomach fries both. There is nothing more beautiful than the act of carrying, or being carried. The mother in the people, the land and the kid, in their leadership. "Those who have ears to hear let them hear!" To err is…hear! He remembers this was what preaching was like growing up in his church. You give a parable, you explain it a little bit, and then you say "ane nzeve dzokunzwa ngaanzwe", "ko asina", that one who doesn't have ears, like the kid on their backs!

And on their backs is monster kid
Of their own making, the little Hitler
So they now carry evil on their backs
A belsen of pain, ridicule, dum-do
Donaldump trump, trumping, dumping
Dumping another act, law, to law
To chase, to erase, to dehumanize, to
Desecrate, innocent DACA immigrants
In the name of "right" to belong
To belong where, are we not all on Mamma Earth!

This has always troubled him. It seems like there are several planets on mother earth, and anyone from outside "our country" is alien, like those dreamy monsters from a planet of our fantasies, millions of light years away. It's as if a new born baby decides where to be given birth to, where to grow up. Is there anyone who has ever paid money to buy a country, a continent? Man professes to be free, to have freewill, to be better than animals and birds, yet he is a prisoner to his rules. A bird never cares about passports, rights to fly, to cross borders, to make home, to live, to eat, to be a bird. Yet to be human is supposed to be divine!

But their Hitler will decide their humanity
Will deny them their humanity
For he says he doesn't give a fig about them.
And closer home, in my household
It's the election games; Raila Vs Uhuru
Railing down the Celebrations- for another day
In the lands of giants, waThiong'o, Mugo,
Maraga is "The River Between Them."
And in my next household, southerly
The legendary fights, Mugabe Vs Tsvangirai
Brews another clay-pot beer for us as
We jostle, push, heckle, tackle for a gulpfull (fill)
Will Makarau be Maraga (the Ides of Kenya)?
And deeper south, Mzanzi yezingoma.
Zuma, *not* that Zulu "umshini wami" dance boy!
Squares it off with Ramaphosa, and waits,
Plot(ty) Zille and the mischievous Malemania boy
It's Africa baby, it's crazy, fun, wacky…
Wonderful!

"You mess one man, you got us all…
The boys of fall", Kenny Chesney belts
This springy Country and Western song

In, deeper, inside this room

****

It's 6 o'clock now, he is still in bed, watching
The heavy shadows of the night's colours
Descending, from outside the room, to inside
He is in bed, its 8 o'clock, clocking sleeping
And in this room he listens to the-
Soft hushing, shushing, swishing- slashings
Of the little oozing shower waters

As the shower shivers in the bathroom cubicle whilst
George, his cousin, takes a bath. He is sleeping-sitting,
sleeping-thinking, sleeping-listening to music; Choral,
Catholic Zimbabwean music; corralling drums, hosho
and beautiful voices, little cacophony. They share this
place they call home. Home, is to own. Not the whole
place, but only their cottage, the outside structure.
Home is to have a structure. They have been staying in
this cottage for 7 months. Seven months in which he
has been cooped inside himself, in this room.

Seven grandfathers, seven sacraments, seven buttons.
Buttons are the threshold of entry into
The insides of a country, a heaven, a girl
He has been fascinated by the act of unbuttoning
His mind, his brain, this room- now unbuttoned
It's time to let the grandmothers rest

9

Doubt, fear, anger, anxiety... boredom
Back into the horizons of his dreamscapes

7 September 2017

He is in bed, its 11 o'clock, clocking elevensis
It gets warmer, 11 o'clock tea tears his room, now warmy
He finds his human skins, the music of a balmy
Spring, singing songs sweeter, nectar, cinnamon
As he is sometimes out of his cotton skins
It's like a dream you dream of getting out
Of, but never manage to leave
On and on, you are running, running, running
Running is your surname
Running is now you,
it doesn't matter. It never matters, it never mattered
It's in a gate-away car, on foot, horse riding,
A hyena, the cat, the black goat, the bat
Last night it was a car, he kept reaching
For his fares, it had too many zeros
The zeros making laughing Eros signs as they disappeared like
errors,
Reappeared, someone shouts like a drunken god
"Muchena Mountain has fallen inside itself"
There are animals he doesn't know their names
Some have fallen in the hole that was Muchena
Besides him, disappearing and reappearing
Is a girl who recently told him she is taken?
Is pregnant, she lives somewhere in Asia

On that other side of the world his friends from Asia,
on social platforms, are mourning the taking away

11

(murder) of a journalist Gauri Lankesh in India. REAL Journalists are food for politicians. REAL writers are food for the politicians. REAL artists are food for the politicians. And immigrants are food for politicians. Outsiders are food for politicians. ALIENS are food for politicians. Rohingyas in Myanmar are food for the major tribes, Rohingyas in Myanmar are food for the UN, Rohingyas in Myanmar are food for the USA, Rohingyas in Myanmar are food for the Myanmar politicians, some whom they (the Swedish Mafia House, not the ...singers) have awarded their purported great prizes, ennobling and enabling them to glut, gut without stop, stay, as they call, keen and keep their Noble eyes innards.

8 September 2017

It is 2 o'clock, he is in bed, ill
Aung San Suu Kyi is a keyhole
He thinks we need to find the keys
And these keyholes, to unlock the locks
That have created the Would Be(s) locks:
The would be Nobel winners not noble
The would be writers who only write- never create
The would be artists who only paint- are not artists
The would be singers who only sing- they have voices
The would be musicians who only make noise- they have
instruments
The would be teachers who only have papers-
The would be leaders who are only politicians-
And the list is endless....

We need to weed these vultures out. They have to be
pushed into the dark forests where they came to- from,
so they stay with others of their likes, fletching each
other, feeding off each other, fighting off each other,
and how good will be our world without these! He is ill,
he feels ill every day. He has bile today, it weakens him.
He has a headache today, it is like some warm steamy
air is being blown into his mind through his noseholes.
His head is on low-stoking fire. He is ill without being
ill, of his world. Its shit, its bile, its bullshit he sees every
day. He takes a breather, drops his pen, and nurses his
head for another day.

******

2 February 2018

Inner-city, in set-squares of noise
Bubbling drones of noise, honking cars
Loud voices, hawkers, pedestrians, buildings
Inner-city buildings of a noisy language
Hot-speaks, hot-structures, hot-forms
And hot-holds the city in squares
Right across Lillian Ngoyi's four ways
Plodding traffics deeps into the heart of the city
Residential flats, some old, scaling paints, some new pains
Dominates his eastern view, like those pillars
Huge prehistoric pillars of brown rocks
He is cooped in the fifth floor of a flat across
Browns, shades of brown, off-whites, whites, greens, screams
Flat on his butt, flat on his stomach, he observes
Park Gardens is the name of his flat
To the other side, in Jeff Masemola street
Is Burgers Park, verdant beautiful lawns?
Trees, flowers, structures; it forms a green machine
That circles back into Lillian Ngoyi Street
Tall jacarandas, acacias…, provide a canopy shade
To those walking in the sidewalks, adds to
And contrasts the tall residential structures across
It is a "worked beauty" landscape
And in idolizing these green souls
He has mind to sketch a drawing of, paint it
But it is daylight, no moon lights his mind

He is hot in words, the room faces the sun
The east gapes large on top of the flats
With cotton white soapy clouds foaming
Sprinkled with faint fluffs of white dust flour
Bored in blue, are lakes lakeing between them
Oh please shut up! I have made it a word…
And in the flat gravity wills you down
You want to look down to the street
Down to the home for humans
To live in a flat is to be a wingless bird
To share the atmospherics of city birds
To drink into dreams that flies high
To live in a flat is to live
In a home away from the home you hate
Or a home away from the home you love
He is beat! Maybe a home in a home
That is *almost* home, but not quite so
Right across he sees people walking in
The corridors, the walkways, rooms, on top of the flats
Are assortments of satellite dishes like ears
Of owls that hears the voices in the winds
In Jeff Masemola Street, a flat, two flats off
The corner of Lillian Ngoyi, it has two
Human like figures that seems sited
On chairs, drinking tea, as they discuss elevation
To stay in elevation is to stay close to dreams
And a guy in blue shirt and a red b/cap
Steals his attention, right across
The guy watches the south, he watches the guy

The guy shifts to the north, he follows the guy
Bores deep into the heart of the city
And then the guy climbs steps into
A small hut on top of the flat
This hut always seduces his eyes
He has seen people coming out smitten
And people going in, like termites
Into a hole within, in this flat
He knows what your mind thinks is happening in this hole
Until someone tells you it's a washing room!
And then his eyes scan again, sees sameness,
Looks inside the room, sees sameness,
Decides into the insides, sees nothingness

3 February 2018

A BLANK PIECE OF PAPER

A blank piece of paper is torture
When the mind is untorched by the touches
Of a writer welding a pen, lighting
This pen becomes a sword of pain
Piercing to blankness the writer's mind
Burning it blue flames of the mire

A blank piece of paper burns
It burns like white tree hunger
A blank piece of paper invites
The pen to start dancing rhythmically
To the sounds in the mind mimic-ally
Wielding the pen like swordstick tines
Of a sword dulled and flattened by time

A blank piece of paper seizures
The mind into small paper pieces
Shredded, scissor-ed, razor-ed, tiny tinybits
Haphazard twits of an inchoate spirit
Who throws the pieces into the blue

A blank piece of paper tells
Tall tales better than a pen tells
In its vast, silent white space untold
Are tales waiting to be detailed?

By the blueshifts of the tolling pens

A blank piece of paper is
A blank piece of mind to
A blank piece of paper
Ay man, I give up!
This blank piece of paper beats me!

4 February 2018

The sky is still cotton lumps of clouds but scored with dusty dirty greyness. The grey of mackerel fish and cigars smoke. These lumps seem arranged one on top and another below, synchronicity, impossible syncopation, the possible leaving gaps between the lumps- that look like blue lakes. He faces the south east part of the view. It's a number of structures, same height juxtaposed, interposed, arranged like those clouds lumps without gaps, lake gaps, its solid symmetrical, precise, the building to the immediate south east, a little lower than the others, behind it is structured in a movie style interesting sort of way. It is angular with windows of different flats overlooking each other. This means you can strike conversation with your next door over the windows. You can look into the inner worlds of your neighbor's without having to ask. His flat is straight plain, he can only see into Lilian Ngoyi and Van der Welt streets, not into the next room. He has to go to the passage way to see, to meet new people, to converse outside of his flat. There is no need! Seeing in, seeing out, seeing has no end.

10 February, 2018

My heart is up for sale

Pay half price for it now
If I had two I would sell,
"dollar for two", or "two for dollar"
Whichever tickles your fancy!
My heart is up for sale
I don't need to keep it
It has been too expensive to keep
So please pay half price for it
Throw me a quarter for it
I will sell it to you
My heart is up for sale
Don't worry about change
If you want it, pay whatever you have
I can't keep it anymore
For it has been of little use
And of more pain and strife
It's the cheapest pound of flesh
You can ever get from any butchery
You can braai it with a beer
Grind it with a little pasta
Enjoy every fibre, every fat.
You can boil it into broil
Season it, serve it with steamed rice

You can feed it to your prof,
Cat- the lab student, knowledge;
Study its pipes, valves, fibres
You can burn it in fire
Send its smoke to the rain gods
To bleed tears for our cape.

****

Between places

To refuse yourself to feel things is to refuse yourself to breathe yet you are breathing. To be unaware of yourself breathing. To not know of the warmth and moistures of your breath. To not know of the human sounds of life. To refuse yourself to feel things is to not see the sky above the building across your windows. To hear noise below you as pollution. To refuse yourself to feel things is to live between places. To be in the east until it begins to feel like east, it takes you 4 seasons for you to figure out where the sun is coming from and going back to come back at that same position, but before the fourth season, you found yourself to the west. Sekelgrass music is lost to the sounds of traffic passing through Sekelgras road off to…you don't know. To refuse yourself is to live for a month in the west and move to the centre, to see a person and not to talk to them. To see a spirit that sees you not. In a matchbox abdomen, you refuse to call this home. Before the west becomes the sounds and vowels that you use to describe home, the horizons trails off as you move to the centre. But the actual events happened vice versa, west to east…but we all know we artistically would start with east to west to lend credence to the theory of the eastern myth. Don't sweat! It is what it has become…the centre. To refuse to feel things is to stay in the centre that doesn't hear you, yet like the heart it should, must hear you. You know the centre has lived inside you for a year now, you still don't hear it, it doesn't hear you too. It doesn't see you. To live between places is to be a fish that learns to live out of water to learn the first word of its alphabet. To refuse to feel anything is to refuse to hear the last gasp of a dying fish denied of its earth. To live between places is to subtract everything until even a negative is not a number. That's the primary school of living between places, it's like 1 minus 2 equals *it cant!*

My heart is not up for sale

I don't want to, no
I am not going to, no
I will never do that, no
No, I am not up to it
No, I don't want to
No, my heart is not for sale
I want to stay safe, yes
I want to not feel, yes
I want to not love, yes
Yes, I will stay closed
Yes, I will hide my heart
Yes, I will not allow it
To melt from warmth, no
To hear the songs of birds, no
To hear the smell of flowers, no
No, it will not hear her song
No, it will not hear her voices
No, it will not see her colours
I will cut it into pieces, yes
I will pour it hot water, yes
I will burn it in fire, yes
Yes, I will blow its ashes into air
Yes, I will smoke its ashes
Yes, I will drink its ashes
I will get drunk on its demise, yes
I won't ever hear it, no

I will live in peace, yes
No, I don't want to
Yes, I am not going to
No, I will never do that again!

14 February 2018

Adate ture eee tuu…, tuu pee, zhuum, pee pee
The taxi touts, the vehicles, the people
In actual fact he is saying ihambe eMenleni (Menlyn)
Are the sounds that dominates his east
Lilian Ngoyi and Jeff Masemola talks
Of the wars, now so far off, fought,
Unfought with Van der Welt
and Jacob Mare now quieted
In our memories, ask Andries Bekker.
He is just an interloper, wanderer
The *Mutakanthram* of Al Maari's *The Epistle
of Forgiveness*. To forgive himself,
He wanders unseen in the city
Into its noises, angers, distrusts
Like the proverbial wandering chew
Whose tentacles were cut by the north beast
He is a eunuch in a city of beauties
His heart refuses to glow, his body,
He means his testicles coagulates
His mind over-records, re-records, un-records
Like a chameleon in awe of its powers
His eyes sees things, sees them not
Sees the east, sees inside, in the clutter
That swamps, logs, sands, quicksilvers,
Pull him in, deeper and deeper
Into nothingness that he sees not
He walks the city, he breathes the city

He makes the city, but it doesn't make him
Adate ture eee tuu…, tuu pee, zhuum, pee pee
The tout calls for fares off to the east he stayed
Menlyn, Garsforntein, Constantia Park
Water Glen, Waterkloof, Hazelwood, is white
Jeff Masemola, Lillian Ngoyi, Thabo Sephume, is black
That clangs him, mobs him, assaults him
Insults him with life out there he can't be
In the inner tunnels of his mind he rests
He is like a ghost trawling inner wastelands
He is a ghost known by its smell.
He doesn't smell himself like a skunk
No one sees the shapes, the shadows, his shapes
He is August's black storms on the skies
Blinking electric blackness blotting
Burnt cities, burned cities, burnt, burning
Whirling in chaos, broken buildings, bones
Strings that are words without meanings
Fingernails, toenails, so much hair. It grows
He has allowed it to grow on his head
When he stayed in the white east
More hair that covers him burns, pull off
From the widow's peak that crater his head
Animated, bright, fierce and shinning like a heart
Nothing is wasted, everything is wasted
Something is retained, always changing shapes
On his way to the next brief shelter
The next campsite, the next ruin,
The ruin of him in this city

******

He could hear them coming before he could see them. He learned the art of hearing the sounds they are not even making as they come. In the east- almost a year ago, she came, talked to him. He talked to her. She was a Venda girl, tall, curvy, lovely... A home he wasn't sure he wanted to drink in its shades, waters, food, to sit in, to sleeps in. She was a church mate, Sundays, two Sundays. Two Sundays they talked, two Sundays he couldn't take her digits. If she had her way she could have but she had her ways, she couldn't just tell him to call her. Another Sunday later, he was in the east and for some months he thought of her.

Like brutal weather, bootlicker poets.

But some few weeks (it's a year) later he heard her coming in before he could see her. She worked at postnet Menlyn. A sweet beautiful *coloured* girl. He worked on the internet from the postnet's computers. So from day one she came and talked to him. He talked, she smiled, left her counter post, probed, left, came back to sit on the next computer, always attuned to him, his shapes. But he stayed inside, getting touched, torched inside. He is an inside person.

4 October 2018

To move, to unloose, to lose, to use, to misuse, to choose to move into spaces, to be in spaces of differing climes, dusts, humans, people, statehood, he meant villagehood. We are village people, yet we stay close to the wanderer's spirit inside us. To touch people and not to be touched, to be torched by people, to live at the first edge of the night, when already everything around you is approaching the second edge of the night. He is suddenly into his old haunt. Not really the place he knows like the back of his mind, but it's the same hand, place. He sees, in fact he looks into, does he see... the human noise all around him? It is a crazy world, mad world where humans like him have stayed behind in, in trying to live. Trying is the only art here, in this place. Otherwise the music should have stopped, but it plays. It plays for the people, but not for him. He sees them dancing to it, he doesn't know how to dance anymore after un-participating in the dances for nearly two years now. He is a spectator, a blind spectator, deaf, dump, him who uses his other senses to feel for the music...only to see there is only their dancing. How can that one who doesn't see, sees. He gets to the intersection at Cripps Road, the coca cola place on his way to the heart of this myth they call H-Town. It is a two roads intersection, it is packed, jammed with traffic that have interlocked into each other, and nothing is moving...like his mind throughout these poetic journals of his life.. his existence. There is no law to law it up here, at this intersection of life. Its survival of the canniest, the craziest, the kombiest drivers. This is the sound of the music he sees them dancing to. You live or die, you kill or be killed, you steal or be stolen, the knowledge of life!

****

To know a thing you have known before is to relearn a letter in the alphabet, *aaa, eee, iii, ooo, uuu,* have I become a vowel, he asks himself. Or a letter? What letter, he remembers in his lazy couch lifestyle in his early twenties he used to call himself, A.B.C...*Another Black Creation*..., he must have stolen it from somewhere, for it was that time when one wanted to sound different, and unless you are really different you can only sound different by stealing. He doesn't recall. Black is the thing he has known before, it is a thing that is on him, not in him. To learn that your skin is the colour that you know it is not is the first lesson to blackness every black kid learns like that first letter in Another Black Creation, A. To be colour blind is to accept a colour that you are not, to call yourself green when you are yellow. To be colour blind is to see colours in not seeing colours. Be careful of where *not* is in this sentence. He tanks his thoughts

29 April 2019

Blankness is not a colour? It took him October, November, December, January, February, March…, now April endish to figure out the colour of blankness of his mind, 6 months jotting nothing. Nothing is something in writing. He remembers in his previous writings somewhere saying that the great art in writing is not writing, not to wield the pen. So these past 6 months have really been the art you will find in his artwork, when he was silent, when he was nothing. No colour is a colour too. A blank year, yet *thimgs* are happening. His job is to *thimg* up *thimgs*. Things that he doesn't/don't feel like writing. Silence is life. And today's art is in the honking of cars and the noises of Lillian Ngoyi Street, which has the usual dappled colours. The air is soft, cool, autumny beauty. They are approaching another *cruel cruel* winter. Winter is a season for the insides of writing. He is an insider, and inside something always enters. No it entered some February day. Didn't he tell you the story or art is in what he doesn't write? He has been spending time with her, cooped in the room he shares with a cousin. She is an old friend from back when they were in their village to the north of the great river. A girl he saw growing up. She is now his heart like things that grows, glows, clots…and refuse to go… he knows this one will stay even after he stops seeing her, before she comes…

Dawn at Chigovanyika: 29 September 2019

Walking the dusty streets,
dawn stripes its waking colours
Naked colours, ashy grey nudity
Grey rays, chalk greys, sandy grain roads
Of Chigovanyika of boxes, matchbox businesses, box houses
Crammed together, inside roads like a cartographer's winded
thoughts
What she told of this land shouldn't have been our vision
Of offish brown, greying, cackling skins, worn out clothes
Eve's angels oils this dirty with their butts, socks
Hands, legs, tables, chairs, stools, stalls
And the counters of cardboard boxes, goods arranged
For the early bird that doesn't catch the worms
Human effigies that look like people
The people he had seen in another world
Before he came back to this mad humans' world
Of calves ceaselessly milking their dead mothers
"4bond, 4bond, 4bond kuTown makagara"
The strength in his voice is thick with method
The taxi tout calls out to the meandering
Line that waits for 2bond "Zupco Diaries"
Tanaka Chidora jots, blogs, in his Zupco Diaries
In the inner paper and pen, the maps inside
He (the narrator has taken over) looked into his (Tanaka) eyes and
saw his own distorted reflection. *Explanation poetry!*
As he sits waiting, watching for the 2bond Zupco buses

This man has been here long enough to answer his own questions
"3bond, 3bond, 3bond kuTown makamira"
"Vabereki ngatiswendedzane kumashure tiende kuTown"
Packing up his taxi, to the tout they are just bricks
One on top of the other, breathing in tandem
It reminds him of the taxi tout of yesteryear in Jeff Masemola street
In that world of people, the "ihambe iMenleni" taxi tout
Streaming from his balcony windows in a flat in Lilian Ngoyi street
This new old town waits for him with minted coin hunger
So he takes the 4bond taxi to be in step with time
Tanaka takes the 4bond taxi to be in step with
His students waiting at that olden hilltop of learning
On the greener stripes of this minted town.

Svosve, Zengeza afternoon: 20 October 2019

The old man whose heart gave up
Like the quiet that has left this ghetto's streets
As cars, bicycles, pushcarts line its edges
The old man who conquered an accident
That took his wife, children, a friend
He has now traded ceremony for distance from us
Championing for us a winter of hot ceremony
The old man whom he used to joke with
Buried his name and the path he chose
He wants to dig out the dirt where his seed came to rest
He wants, he wants, he wants to burn it
To ash and forget the laughter they had together
The old man who was his father's friend
Begun to hum a tune of a trail song
Of wear and war and waste
The wife of a friend he grew up with in the streets
Eased away from what we knew of her
His sister's boyfriend of over two decades ago
She cannot wait for time to touch her with old ways of loving
The father of his neighbour, his mother,
Beginning with a riddle of silence
The old church girl he was friends with since she was 12
Eaten by bp at 20, he whispers her name *Karen, Karen, Karen....*
Who said angels have white wings only?
The tens he hasn't seen since he returned from the world of people

He looks around himself to see their shadows
He looks inside himself to hear their voices
An open mouthed roar containing secrets he cannot tell

Zengeza 2 Shopping Centre: 24 October 2019

The things that avoided him the last three years
Walks with him on his way to the shops
The things his eyes are seeing again
Black tarred roads, virginal coloured buildings
Soft full bodies, sweet white smiles, chocolate skins
Replaced by sandy offish grey gravel roads
Crackling walls, soot, soiled, decaying colours
Craggy hard skeletal bodies, yellow black smiles, ivory brownish
khakish skins
As hunger has taken a lotus position on their frames
These are the thingish humans of his world
The humus in the box houses, broken gates, doors, rotting
Windows, dry water tapes, dark bodings of no electricity
The long endless queues, *come back 2008*, the walks
With containers of water, the littering, the hunger
On their faces, hands, minds for freedom, for food
Marching, the march in open prisons for streets
You will meet him in this ground, in these methods
In the high tide and bask of the sun
In the ebb and flow of these thingish humans
In the sides of the walkways, the wares, food...
Fish, tomatoes, veggies, fruits, foreign currency...
Books, meat, clothes, cars, humans, humans...
Hallos, calls out to the ebb of humans pouring
From every opening to the surrounding box houses
Zengeza 1, 2, 3, 4, 5 to Seke Unit A, B, C, D, G, H, J, K, L, M , N,

O, P
Numbers and alphabets names this place
To St Mary's, Manyame Park, Nyatsime...
And at night under the moonlight of the heat of the departed sun
In miniskirts, skimpy dresses, polished, painted faces
Near the electricity place, at the new complex
Are women of the night selling their human tomatoes
To the lies that greedily satiates imagined hungers
The lies that soothes imagined horrors
To the lies that pass for people's legs
As the moon speaks in riddles
She knows, she knows, she knows the wind it blows
The spirits in the wind weighs a million arrows her way

29 October 2019

We will all be back in the streets

We will all come back home
The wind had spread us hither, thither
The rains grew us roots, root us in
Soils that housed our little souls far from home
We were crops, we made fruits
We enriched these soils with our toils
Some won't find the wind to carry them home
Some winds have carried them too far
So far the winds have broken them into chaff
Some winds have stored them in dry caves
Some winds have thrown them into the seas, oceans
To become fodder for the ocean markers
Those who will find their way home
Will find ashes for homes they burned to get away
Some will find hunger, some will befriend thirst
Some will sink wells on the ashes
Some will dry out into ash due to thirsty
Some will reclaim, recreate, rekindle, remake
New bodings out of the homes they left
We will all be back in the streets
The girls who had left to new homes
With the fruits of their wombs in the streets
The girls who never left the streets
The boys who never left the streets

Living with parents, with grandees
In the same homes they never left
Are now the street in the streets
We will all be back in the streets
The girls we have loved more than love itself
The boys we could have loved
We will all be back in the streets
Teaching the fruits of our wombs
How to survive enough to return
Someday into the streets broken, broken like us
To have survived the streets is the new Moses
It is the hot language of Moses in the desert
The streets have the power to gobble up
The strongest, the weakest, the strangest, the prettiest...
All those girls and boys
The streets swallowed and chewed
We will all be back in the streets

23 November 2019

The First "F" in Zimbabwe is Fuck[ed] up

Fuck up to tribalism disguised as nationalism
All lives leach off before they are lived
Fuck up to tribalism disguised in name changes
The fatigue with Zimbabwe's politics has killed us like ponies
Fuck up to tribalism disguised in big words
I mean fuck up to tribalism couched in academic jargon
Fuck up to tribalism disguised as consciousness
Fuck up to tribalism disguised as forced unity
There is no unity in suppression
There is no unity in annihilation
There is no unity in falseness
Fuck up to tribalism sold around as truth
Truth that is false double-spectacled togetherness
Fuck up to tribalism that yokes and yolks dry the country's soul
Fuck up to tribalism the news gatherers sell
Fuck up to tribalism the establishment upholds
Fuck up to tribalism disguised as looting
Fuck up to tribalism the feeding maggots hold onto
Fuck up to this Zezuru, Korekore and Karanga tribalism
Your new stooge Save Us, is a toddler's optimism
Grafted into war plans from old discarded maps
Of G40's divinities grinning in the wings
All leaves now grin reporting to their invisible roots
Fuck up to a nation of minion minds

That aggregates around in small circles
Never to taste the make-believe music of the rectangle
Fuck up to the tribal anger in this pen
To call out against tribalism is to be tribal
The mountain of me has molten into monstrous sands
Fuck up to the tribal minds reading this poem
Fuck up to you for pushing me into this tribal diatribe
Fuck up to a Zimbabwe of two tribes
Dear Save Us, Dear Constant On, Dear Emercy On
What happened? Juridical hubris, banished structure
All your works, but you, are decaying
Fuck up to a Zimbabwe of liars, wimps
Fuck up to this tribal poverty, hunger
Fuck up to this tribal democrazy
Fuck up to tribalism disguised as military demoncracy
I coughed up a failure in the middle of the coup
Trying to put power into nubs, structure, parts
This is puke cut into small eruptions
Look closely into its built-in ways, fluffy
The fluff structure, the fluff regime
The precarious government that discards its people
Dear Constant On, when a hen starts eating its eggs
It won't stop to think of the taste
Laugh now as your men are busy on us
We will stand quiet when they are busy on you
There is a soldier waiting for your mother
Fuck up to this tribal rule of law
Fuck up to this tribal suited rulership
Give me my bow and arrow, my tribal dressing

I will Hong Kong the pegs of my portion of this land
There is no nation where there is no sense of happiness
I want to see a Ndebele presidency, a Manyika presidency
I want to see a Matoko presidency, a Xhosa presidency
Enough time has existed for all of us to happen!
Dear Save Us, Dear Constant On, Dear Emercy On
Own up to your tribal Herr Hitlerian IDs
Revel in your tribalism Herr Hitler's Chihuahuas
Suppress, cajole, kill, rule your tribal monarchs
Write tons of verses, prose, poetry in opposing tribalism
Sing of a nation that lies deep into your tribal organs
Underneath your tribal markers
Dear Emercy On- true life is things in the room
You think the things are thingless or a drain
You are fully aware of the referent here, the collective?
Nouns becoming verbs cuffed to pronouns
Tribalism is as worse as corruption
Tribalism is as worse as human rights abuse
Tribalism is as worse as imposition of sanctions
Tribalism is as dangerous as a virus
Tribalism is as worse as racism
Tribalism has resulted in extinguishing pogroms
Tribalism has destroyed the workplace
Tribalism has mismanaged Zimbabwe
Tribalism has milked people dry
Tribalism has stunted Zimbabwe's growth
Tribalism has dispersed Zimbabweans hither and thither
Tribalism has made her children wander blindly
Don't tell me to see what I am not looking at

Don't tell me to look at what I am not seeing
Show me something new that I am not seeing
See- my heart is now made up of sands-
It slides, slips, collapses:
Shapelessly, yellowish, grainy.

We are not beyond words

We are not beyond words, we are before words
Blood rivers in us, romanticizes the hour hand
Moving closer to that which we must touch
Touching that which we shouldn't be close to
Cruel, possessive, incendiary, broken, begotten, kindness
Touches that which we shouldn't get close to
Touches that which we shouldn't touch
Without getting closer to it
The mound we sit on is lined with the thing
That we shouldn't get close to
And we are holed in that which we shouldn't touch
When touch is all of our being
Our black blood sips into that which we should touch
Into that which we shouldn't touch
It senses that which we should get close to
In the sloughing rivulets of the coming dark thing
There are roads that connect us to other places
Sites, paces, cities, infinities, homes of expressions that houses
Rooms through rooms, moving- we are before words
We are not beyond words!
We go home in our partner's arms, between the four walls
Or the empty blanket of Grandma's Helen
Whose lower ends no one can fold back together
We plant corn, eat fruits, meat, veggies
Wipe away the smoldering waters with our dry hands
Make songs, music, sing, dance, dance

44

Talk; tell stories, jokes, laugh, push off
That dark thing, before that dark thing comes
We are not beyond words, we are before words.

I think it's a combination of these 19 and 20s in Covid 19: 20 March 2020

Dec 2019, the wind found its wings
I could give this wind a heart, if you like
We called this wind Corona Virus Disease: Covid 19
As it gathered all the rainclouds, and
Rained on us, the invasive waters
We were left aghast at 5000 felled trees
We were left at the edges of sense
And now, a week later, 10000 trees are down
With tens, hundreds of thousands on the way
As millions will flow in this Wind River
This is the river of our silent departing

The river soughs through her reeds
As the wind whistles through hemmed
Skirts of the approaching winter's valley
The dark and lonely winter coming
Drifting on the shoulders of this wind
Rolling up residual clouds our way
Under the feverish last sun of a departing autumn
The last death stinks to the heavens and back
As her pounding silences echoes
A snooty refrain in my timid heart

Despite, all along, absence of an inspired wind
We forgot to water ourselves in the insides
And our biggest mistake was to interrupt

The wind whilst it was napping and dozing
Now the wind travels vastness into our future
As the river despise us, disperse us
Each to his or her own mistakes

Our lungs burn, crackles like Kalahari
Baked, sinuous, mapped, dry
We offer our faces to the blows of the wind
The huffing-puffing, tissue world, the weighty fear, the grunts
See the vapour, the sanitizers, the sweat, the endless cleaning
If only cleaning could delete us from ourselves?

We were so selfish to think haunting was ours alone
Yet all that lives shares death
Adroitly, a crow, a doe, a bat, a deer's
Anus strangles us, necklessly, shapelessly, endlessly
Death is lean, proud, and busy
Has gathered every use of retribution
Chai, we thought it's an eastern joke
Mocking the old oaking tree
We are now hoping, praying
For a lighthouse that dapples this darkness
As haunting is now working on us

In our social distancing closures
In these cosmologies of silence
After 10000 trees were felled
Our today is a cage
Our tomorrow is another cage

We need so many safe words
One to decide if today we still light the candle for the other
Another to start workman-like copulation
One to be quiet, another to give each other way
One to ask for salt, another to ask for pepper...
Unfortunately "no" is no longer one of the words
Never is not a safe word; It means
It now means, always- hiding in our closures
No one is excluded from the knowledge
Of the roundness of this home
If you still want to say never
You should now say home
If you still want to say no
You should come home

There is a woman

There is a woman he had to outgrow in his mind
The woman made in the wide forest acres of the eastern
villages
The woman implanted in the walkways he plodded yesteryear
The woman that cut him into the first pieces of gold
The woman who moltened his flesh with fire
The woman whom life always refuses to stay
For if she had stayed he won't be the human he is

There is a woman who was flies on his first wound
The woman who was committed to fest on his numbing
wounds
The woman who wanted her shadows to talk and cut deep
The woman who hardened the wounds as she prodded
The woman whose shadow wafted as the years wane
The woman he doesn't recall like the feelings of that first
wound

There is a woman who didn't come even though she came,
not that way!
The woman who didn't go even though she left
The woman who didn't stay even though she stayed
The woman who unoccupied so much space
The woman who failed to hold onto so much time
The woman who negated place and time, deleted by place and
time

There is a woman who has arrived on his doorstep
The woman he has waited a lifetime to arrive
The woman so many wasted away to prepare for
The woman he will allow to unlock the doors

The woman whom his insides, like a ship, she will dock in
To stay until another paradise calls him away

Something is happening to me

Something happened to me as they told me
There was this novel beast that takes and takes
The old, young, not so young old, adults
Something happened to me when they told me
I need to stay Indoors, in closures, all alone
In my room unawaiting for its tempest heat

Something has been happening to me
As I have commuted with the four walls
For 4 months, exhausting winter off its cold dresses
Late autumn is now a memory of fear fermenting
That the beast would still find its way to me

Something happened to me every time I had
To leave my four walls to find food
Something happened to me when the law man
Told me I can't go past this block or
That I can't walk off to buy food, I can't fetch water
I can't go past the blockage to the city
I can't walk without a mask to mask my fears
I have to constantly clean my hands
I can't hug, touch, tease, kiss, love…
I can't allow myself to have feelings
I can't feel the lover's heat as it warms my fingers
I can't dance, laugh, smile, stomp with life

Something is happening to me when it hits home
When the wild beast stalks past the gates
To do a lotus position indoors, knowing it's in every cup,
Plate, pan, stove, spoon, jar, jag, fork

Stove, spoon, jag, jar, pan, plate, fork,
Waiting and waiting for me

Something is happening in me
As my brother and I share this home
Waiting and waiting,
With my brother in the next room
Waiting and waiting,
With my next door friends
Waiting and waiting
In the streets that I still walk indoors
Waiting and waiting
In the foodshops, foodstalls, foods
That I need to survive to see it out
Something is happening to me
Jailed by this animal I can't see

You Weren't Watching Me

You weren't watching me
watching you when you were a sapling sprout
You weren't watching me
Touching you with the hands of hearts

You weren't watching me
Latching onto the bright rays of your youthhood
You weren't watching me
Watching you dancing on life's dancefloors

You weren't watching me
Idolizing you whilst sleeping, sinning
Awake, you weren't watching me
Watch you leaving me so many times

And waiting for you to come back again and again
You weren't watching me watching you
Watching me
The shadow that watches you watching me
Watching you leaving me.

Mmap New African Poets Series

If you have enjoyed *Between Places* consider these other fine books in **New African Poets Series** from *Mwanaka Media and Publishing:*

I Threw a Star in a Wine Glass by Fethi Sassi
Best New African Poets 2017 Anthology by Tendai R Mwanaka and Daniel Da Purificacao
Logbook Written by a Drifter by Tendai Rinos Mwanaka
Mad Bob Republic: Bloodlines, Bile and a Crying Child by Tendai Rinos Mwanaka
Zimbolicious Poetry Vol 1 by Tendai R Mwanaka and Edward Dzonze
Zimbolicious: An Anthology of Zimbabwean Literature and Arts, Vol 3 by Tendai Mwanaka
Under The Steel Yoke by Jabulani Mzinyathi
Fly in a Beehive by Thato Tshukudu
Bounding for Light by Richard Mbuthia
Sentiments by Jackson Matimba
Best New African Poets 2018 Anthology by Tendai R Mwanaka and Nsah Mala
Words That Matter by Gerry Sikazwe
The Ungendered by Delia Watterson
Ghetto Symphony by Mandla Mavolwane
Sky for a Foreign Bird by Fethi Sassi
A Portrait of Defiance by Tendai Rinos Mwanaka
When Escape Becomes the only Lover by Tendai R Mwanaka
ويَسهَرُ اللَّيلُ عَلَى شَفَتي...وَالغَمَام by Fethi Sassi
A Letter to the President by Mbizo Chirasha

Righteous Indignation by Jabulani Mzinyathi:
Blooming Cactus By Mikateko Mbambo
Rhythm of Life by Olivia Ngozi Osouha
Travellers Gather Dust and Lust by Gabriel Awuah Mainoo
Chitungwiza Mushamukuru: An Anthology from Zimbabwe's Biggest Ghetto Town by Tendai Rinos Mwanaka
Pressed flowers by John Eppel
This is not a poem by Richard Inya
Because Sadness is Beautiful? by Tanaka Chidora
Of Fresh Bloom and Smoke by Abigail George
Shades of Black by Edward Dzonze

Soon to be released

Best New African Poets 2020 Anthology by Tendai Rinos Mwanaka, Lorna Telma Zita, and Balddine Mousa
Denga reshiri yokunze kwenyika by Fethi Sassi
Under African Skies by Yugo Gabriel Egboluche
This Body is an Empty Vessel by Beaton Galafa

https://facebook.com/MwanakaMediaAndPublishing/

Printed in the United States
by Baker & Taylor Publisher Services